MONTROSE

Covenanter, Royalist
and Man of Principle

First published in Great Britain
in Merlins in 1996

Text © Ruth Blackie

Ruth Blackie has asserted her rights under
the Copyright, Designs and Patents Act
1988 to be identified as the author of this
work.

HB ISBN 0 86241 640 X

PB ISBN 0 86241 657 4

Cataloguing-in-Publication Data
*A catalogue record for this title is
available upon request from the British
Library*

Typeset and designed by
Artisan Graphics, Edinburgh

Printed and bound by
Oriental Press, Dubai

The publisher acknowledges subsidy from the Scottish Arts Council
towards publication of this volume

The publishers are grateful to the following organisations and individuals
for permission to reproduce illustrations.

The front cover shows a detail from the portrait of of Montrose by van
Honthorst, reproduced by permission of the Scottish National Portrait
Gallery: *pages 5, 8, 13, 21, 44* Crown Copyright: Royal Commission on the
Ancient and Historic Monuments of Scotland: *page 6* by courtesy of St
Andrews University Library: *pages 7, 34, 39* by permission of the Trustees of
the National Library of Scotland: *page 9* Edinburgh Public Libraries: *pages
10 top, 12 right, 19, 20, 24, 29, 38, 41, 48* Scottish National Portrait Gallery:
pages 10 bottom, 16, 31, 33 National Museums of Scotland: *pages 11 top,
30* The Clann: *page 12 left, 37* by courtesy of the National Portrait Gallery,
London: *page 14* National Museums of Scotland and the Kirk Session of
Greyfriars, Edinburgh: *page 22* by courtesy of His Grace the Duke of Argyll:
page 32 John Scott Adie: *page 35* National Gallery of Scotland: *page 40*
by permission of the Earl of Rosebery: page 47 Miss M Wallace. Every effort
has been made to trace holders of copyright, and we apologise to any
whom it has proved impossible to contact.

CANONGATE BOOKS LTD
14 HIGH STREET EDINBURGH EH1 1TE

MONTROSE

Covenanter, Royalist and Man of Principle

Ruth Blackie

CANONGATE • MERLINS

The Chronology of Montrose's Life

Events in Scotland	The life of Montrose	Events in England

	Events in Scotland	The life of Montrose	Events in England	
1610	Scotland ruled from London by James VI			1610
	1612 attempts to 'Anglicise' church	1612 Montrose born		
1620				1620
		1624–29 student in Glasgow and St Andrews	1625 accession of Charles I	
1630		1632–34 travels on Continent	1629 start of 'Eleven years of Tyranny'	1630
	1633 Coronation of Charles I			
	1637 new Prayer Book			
	1638 Covenant	1638 signs National Covenant		
	1639 Bishops' Wars		1640 Parliament recalled	
1640	1642 revolution: Scots Parliament supports English Parliament	1641 imprisoned by Argyll	1642 Civil War	1640
		1643 campaign starts		
		1645 Philiphaugh		
		1646 Exile		
1650	1651 Charles II crowned	1650 return to Scotland	1649 Charles I executed: Oliver Cromwell named 'Lord Protector'	1650
		1651 execution		
1660	1661 Execution of Argyll	1661 funeral	1660 restoration of Charles II	1660

Chapter One

Montrose's Youth

In 1612 the castle of Auld Montrose saw the birth of James Graham, who later became the fifth Earl and first Marquis of Montrose. His birth probably caused great excitement for his parents John Graham (the fourth Earl) and Margaret.

The Grahams were one of the greatest noble families in Scotland. They already had five daughters, but it was important for them to have a male heir to inherit their estates, which stretched from Mugdock in the west to the prosperous town of Montrose in the east.

As far as we know, the young James had a happy childhood, although his mother died when he was only six. He had the run of the family's estates, and had horses of his own. He was a frequent visitor to the home of his eldest sister, Lilias, who had married Sir John Colquhoun in 1620 and gone to live at Luss, on Loch Lomond.

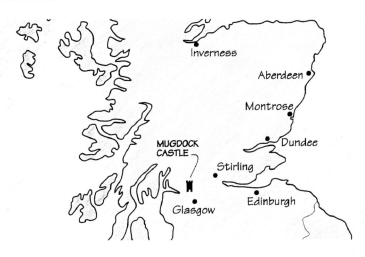

Childhood

Mugdock Castle marked the western point of the Graham Estates, which stretched across the country to Montrose in the east.

When James was twelve years old, he was sent to live in a "great ludgin situat in the citie of Glasgow", to be educated by a tutor. The list of items which he took with him confirms that the boy came from a wealthy family. He had richly decorated coats and suits, silver cups, bedding, ornaments, books, a handgun, and a crossbow set with mother-of-pearl. He was also accompanied by his tutor and two page boys.

Lord James had been in Glasgow for only eighteen months when he was called to his father's death-bed. At the age of fourteen he had become Earl of Montrose and chief of all the Grahams.

Student Days and Marriage

After settling the family's affairs, the young Earl set out for a few years' study at the University of St Andrews. There, it would seem, he had an enjoyable time, not only studying but playing golf or tennis, and hunting and hawking. Two years running he won the Silver Arrow, the top prize for archery. He also enjoyed music.

It is from the accounts of his spending that we know what Montrose did during those years and also something of his personality. Not only did he spend on his pleasure, but he gave generously to others. Every day, he gave to the poor, to porters, to boys who carried his clubs, and to beggars. He sometimes bought books, and once he paid a poet to write verses for him. Sometimes he even paid to get out of his own work. There is an item in the accounts for twenty-nine shillings being paid to "a scholar who writes my Lord's notes in the school".

At the end of July 1629, James Graham's student days ended. He was about to marry Magdalen Carnegie from Kinnaird, the neighbouring estate to Auld Montrose. We know very little about Magdelen, but it certainly would have been accepted for the young Earl to marry the wealthy girl next door. We have no detailed account of the wedding, but almost certainly his new father-in-law laid on a great feast. There would have been huge banquets with fowl, venison and other meats; plenty of wine to drink, and minstrels would have played for entertainment and dancing.

The Silver Arrow Archery Prize awarded to Montrose in 1628.

Chapter Two

How People Lived

Life in 17th-century Scotland was very different from life today.

If a traveller had to cross the Graham estates, from Mugdock in the west to Montrose in the east, progress would be very slow. He would be travelling on foot, or, if he was lucky, on horseback. The journey would probably take nearly a week. There were no roads as we know them, only tracks for carts to be dragged along, and the countryside did not look as it does today. There were no large fields, no fences, no hedges, and very few trees: instead there were many flat bogs which would later be drained and made fertile. Country people lived in *fermtouns* (farm towns), huddles of tiny houses where the only building of any size was the church.

The Lowland Countryside

*Round the fermtoun houses was an area of cultivated land shared by everyone living in the fermtoun. It was divided into strips of heaped-up earth with ditches in between. This was the **runrig** system*

This cultivated area was known as the infield, and oats and bere (barley) were grown here. Beyond the infield lay the outfield, where a few scraggy sheep and cattle grazed.

Coins of Montrose's time.

By modern standards, the houses were hovels. The walls of stone and turf were covered by a thatched roof, and the floor was just earth. Smoke from the fire curled up through a hole in the roof. The whole house must have stank because the people shared it with their animals.

There was not much furniture. People would sit around the fire on stools to eat their food, which was usually brose (a thin gruel or soup). They did not own any of the land. It was all owned by the laird, and they had to pay him rent. Sometimes this rent was paid in money and sometimes it was paid *in kind*, as crops and livestock. When the harvest was bad it was very difficult to pay the rent.

Some lairds had only a small amount of land, but some were noblemen who owned thousands of acres.

A Nobleman's Life

A nobleman like Montrose would have occupied a very large house or a castle, with many servants living there as well as a large family. Inside, the stone walls would be covered with wooden panelling and there would be wooden chairs and tables, wooden platters and spoons. The floors would be covered with straw. The nobility often bought new things from abroad, and they might have have large beds, leather chairs, curtains, mirrors, rugs and silver plates.

The nobility also ate far, far better than their tenants. Here is a description of a nobleman's kitchen while a meal was being prepared for people on a hunt:

> *"There are many kettles and pots boiling and many spits turning and winding, with great variety of cheer; as baked venison; boiled, roast and stewed beef; mutton, goats, kid, hares, fresh salmon, pigeons, hens, capons, chickens, partridge, moorecoots, heathcocks, capercaillies and ptarmigan; good ale, white and red wine and most potent Aquavitae (whisky)."*

A nobleman's house at Craigievar.

Town life in the 17th century was rather different. Most people in Scotland were poor farmers at this time, but roughly ten per cent lived in the burghs. The largest burgh was Edinburgh, the capital, with its castle, royal palace and university. Edinburgh had a population of about 30,000. In 1636, an English traveller, Sir William Brereton, wrote that the capital was a fine city. Here is his description:

> *"The city, which is built upon a hill to give a graceful ascent to the great street which I take to be an English mile long and is the best paved street with boulder stones that I have seen. The channels are very conveniently contrived on both sides of the street; it is the broadest, largest and fairest pavement, to go, ride or drive upon."*

Brereton goes on to describe the stone tenements, five or six storeys high. At the top, wooden additions were built out over the street. The thing Brereton disliked most was the smell: "I was constrained to hold my nose." In fact, it would probably be the smell which we would notice first. There were no plumbing or sewage systems. Water was drawn from pumps in the street and carried by hand to the houses, and excrement was thrown out of the windows on to the street below, with the hope that it would land in the channels or open drains at the side of the road rather than on the heads of passers-by. "Gardy loo," was the warning cry given before the dirt was thrown out.

The Burgh

The Royal Burghs of Scotland in the 17th century.

This map of Edinburgh was drawn by James Gordon of Rothiemay in 1647.

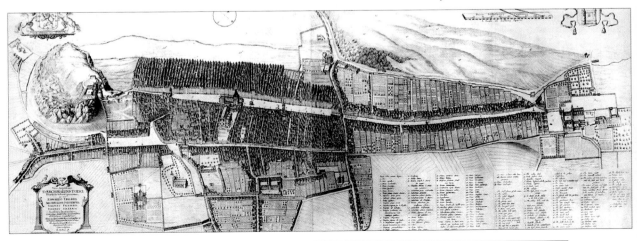

This painting of two young brothers shows the kind of golf clubs which were used in Montrose's time.

Belief and Superstition

But most burghs were much smaller than Edinburgh. Some consisted of a huddle of stone and wooden houses with only a few hundred inhabitants. The finest houses, belonging to the merchants, would lie along the main street, or *gait*, and the poorer dwellings would huddle round the wynds and vennels. The streets were narrow, unpaved lanes, and here again we would probably be struck by the smell and dirt, for at the door of every house was a *midden* or rubbish heap. Outside the town lay the *burgh muir*, for the common grazing of animals, and there might be golf links and targets for archery, as these were popular sports.

There were two types of burgh — royal burghs and burghs of barony. Both had special privileges, granted by the king or the landowner. Royal burghs had the right to trade overseas. They were entitled to their own town councils and could make their own laws. The map on page 9 shows that most of these burghs were on or near the east coast. They traded with towns in northern Europe. Wool, linen and herring were exported in return for imports of iron, wood, flax and wine.

The better-off merchants lived well, in fine stone-built houses, just as the noblemen did. Many of the craftsmen and ordinary people, however, were no better off than the peasants in the fermtouns. Like the peasants, they helped to support themselves by raising cows and pigs.

In the 17th century, almost everyone went to church. Most people were also superstitious; this is shown in their belief in witchcraft. Harmless old women would be put to death because they were 'guilty' of causing a thunderstorm or of killing a calf by magic. Montrose's brother-in-law, Sir John Colquhoun of Luss, was accused of being a warlock (a male witch) because he ran off with his wife's youngest sister, Katharine.

A witch's cursing bone like this one would have provoked great fear amongst people.

The 17th-century Highlander differed from the Lowlander in two ways. He spoke a different language — Gaelic — and he was a member of a clan. *Clann* is a Gaelic word meaning 'children', and all clan members owed allegiance to the chief. The chief could call his clansmen out in time of war, but in return he gave them protection. The clans had often quarrelled amongst themselves, usually over land and cattle. They also largely ignored the rule of the king.

In the Middle Ages the most powerful clan had been the MacDonalds. Until the 15th century their chief had held the title Lord of the Isles and had special powers amongst chiefs. During the 16th century the power of the MacDonalds gradually diminished. Mackenzies took land from them in the north while Campbells, under their chief the Earl of Argyll, took MacDonald lands in Kintyre, Islay and Mull.

James VI tried to impose his rule on the Highlands. He even resorted to warfare in his determination to end, once and for all, the resistance of the clans. By the end of his reign the King had officially brought peace to the Highlands.

But the Highlander remained first and foremost a clansman and the subject of his chief rather than his king. His loyalties lay in his own land and he was more interested in his own clan than in the problems of the king and the government of the country.

The Highlanders were on the whole poorer than the Lowlanders. It was difficult to cultivate the rugged hillsides and wide open moorlands. There was, however, plenty of grazing land, and in summer the people would take their cattle high into the hills for the good pasture. There they would live in stone huts called *sheilings*. In the autumn the little black cattle would be driven to markets in the Lowlands and sold or bartered for food, linen, and other necessities.

This drawing of a sheiling is taken from a book published in 1776.

The Highlands and the Clans

The dress of the 17th century Highlander.

The Highland Landscape

Two Countries with One King

In 1603, the Scottish King, James VI, came to the throne of England as James I. This was because he was the closest living relative of England's Queen Elizabeth — you can see why this was from their family tree. But in the 17th century, Scotland and England were still two completely separate countries with their own governments and laws.

Elizabeth I

James VI

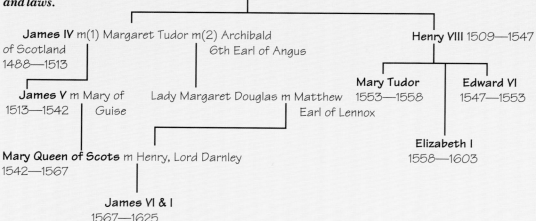

Henry VII 1485—1509

James IV m(1) Margaret Tudor m(2) Archibald
of Scotland   6th Earl of Angus
1488—1513

Henry VIII 1509—1547

James V m Mary of
1513—1542   Guise   Lady Margaret Douglas m Matthew
Earl of Lennox

Mary Tudor   Edward VI
1553—1558   1547—1553

Mary Queen of Scots m Henry, Lord Darnley
1542—1567

Elizabeth I
1558—1603

James VI & I
1567—1625

From the time that King James VI became James I of England, he lived in England. Although when he left Scotland he had promised to come back for one year in three, he only ever visited the country once again, in 1617. He boasted, "Here I sit [in London] and govern with my pen: I write and it is done, and by a clerk of the Council I govern Scotland now which others could not do by the sword." In fact, James very much preferred living in England and would have liked to unite the two countries. He told the English "my intention was always to effect the union by uniting Scotland to England, not England to Scotland."

Chapter Three

James VI, Charles I and Religion

Even after the Union of the Crowns the King could not simply do as he liked, because he did not have total power. There was a Parliament at that time, even though it was not elected in the same way as a modern Parliament. The Scottish Parliament, or *Estates*, contained representatives from the nobility, the burghs and the Church.

However, the King had some power over the Estates because of a committee called the Lords of the Articles. This committee told the Estates what it could discuss and what laws it should pass. In theory, the Estates selected the Lords of the Articles; in practice, the King told the Estates whom to appoint.

This Royal power was resented by some people, but it was over religion that there was real disagreement between James VI and his Scottish subjects.

Government

Virtually everybody in the 17th century went to church. They all accepted that the Church was very important, but not everybody agreed on what kind of church there should be and how it should be organised. The High Kirk of St Giles in Edinburgh was to be the scene of much argument about the right way to worship.

Throughout Europe, the old Catholic Church had just split up, and various Protestant churches had developed in its place (this was called the *Reformation*). Each division of the Protestant church passionately believed that it was the only right one.

Presbyterian Scotland, Episcopalian England

The Scottish Church, or Kirk, had become Presbyterian. This meant that all believers were considered equal and the Church was organised through a series of committees — the Kirk Session, the Presbytery, the Synod and, at the top, the General Assembly, an elected group of ministers and ordinary Kirk members. Presbyterians believed in living a very sober life.

In England the Protestant church had developed rather differently. It had broken away from the Catholic Church under the Pope, but it had remained very similar both in organisation and practice. The monarch was head of the Church, and there were archbishops, bishops and priests below him. The ordinary members had no part in Church organisation.

James's Plans

Even before he became King of England, James VI very much preferred the English system. He wanted an Episcopalian church — that is, one with bishops — in Scotland, because he felt that this would give him more power. In 1600 he persuaded the General Assembly to appoint bishops, and then he gradually increased their authority.

The Presbyterian Kirk in Scotland believed that churches should be unadorned and that services should be kept simple. In the Church of England, services and buildings were more ornate. These communion cups were used in Greyfriars Kirk in Edinburgh.

Now that he had an organisation similar to the Church of England, James wanted the Kirk to appear like the English Church in other ways. In 1617 he declared the Five Articles of Perth. These required people to conform to practices generally considered Roman Catholic, such as kneeling for communion and going to special services at Easter and Christmas.

James VI's policies dealing with the church were unpopular but it was with his son, Charles, that conflict developed into war.

Charles I came to the throne in 1625. He left Scotland at
the age of four and grew up thinking and behaving as an
Englishman. He was a very devout member of the
Church of England and he believed sincerely in the
Divine Right of Kings, a belief that a king is appointed by
God and that his power comes directly from God. This
means that opposition to the king's wishes is opposition
to God's will.

One of the first things that Charles did as King of
Scotland was to demand back from the nobles money
and land that had belonged to the Church before the
Reformation. He wanted the money to improve the pay
of ministers and to decorate the churches. Edinburgh
was driven to bankruptcy by the King's insistence that
the High Kirk of St Giles should be repaired and
adorned, and that a new Parliament House be built.

In 1633, eight years after his accession, Charles I came to
Scotland for his coronation. He angered nobility,
churchmen and peasants alike by ignoring the practices
of the Church of Scotland and using a Church of
England service. Three years later, in 1636, he issued the
Book of Canons (or rules) for the Church. These rules
reorganised the Scottish Church along English lines, and
dictated that the Scottish Church was to use a Prayer
Book written in England by English churchmen.

When this Prayer Book was
first read in St Giles in
1637, it sparked off a riot.
The congregation rose in
tumult. Books and stools
were hurled at the
minister. There's a story
that one woman, Jenny
Geddes, threw her stool,
yelling, "Wha daur say
mass in my lug?"

Charles I's Actions

*The riot in St Giles was recorded
in this drawing soon after it
happened.*

Hardly a soul in Scotland would accept the new Prayer Book. Nobles, burgesses, ministers and peasants all felt that the King had gone too far. Even if some might have agreed to the religious changes, they could not accept that the King had a right to overrule both Parliament and his Church.

News that Charles intended to force the use of the Prayer Book, regardless of the will of the people, led to further rioting. Eventually the King allowed his opponents to form a committee to discuss the matter. But the 'Tables', as the committee became known, went further than this. A General Assembly of ministers, nobles and lairds met in Glasgow. The Moderator was Alexander Henderson, one of the authors of the National Covenant. The Assembly abolished the entire church organisation set up by Charles and his father. The bishops were to lose their jobs. The Five Articles of Perth, the Book of Canons and the Prayer Book all disappeared. Presbyterianism was now re-established.

This was an open challenge to the King. He must either give way completely or fight to keep the bishops. But his belief in the Divine Right of Kings made the bishops necessary for his continuing rule.

The National Covenant.

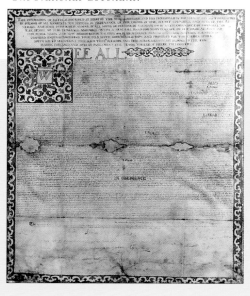

The National Covenant formed 'one band' of the nation of Scotland to defend both the King and the 'true religion'.

Most of it was a list of rules to protect the Presbyterian church. But the people who signed it also stated: "We promise and swear that we shall, to the utmost of our power, with our means and lives, stand to the defence of our dread sovereign, the King's Majesty, his Person and his authority in the defense and preservation of the aforesaid true Religion, Liberties and Laws of the Kingdom."

The Covenanters, as the signatories of the National Covenant were called, swore to defend both religion and King. Was this possible?

Chapter 4

The Bishops' Wars

What had the young Earl of Montrose been doing during these troubled times? And what part did he play in the conflict?

After their marriage, James Graham and his wife Magdalen set up home with her father at Kinnaird. Here two sons were born before Montrose set out in 1632 for the Continent. This was a fashionable thing for wealthy young men to do. He did not go alone — he took with him a valet, grooms, pageboys and a steward. His lifelong friend Tom Sydserf also travelled with him. Sysderf wrote a description of Montrose at this time: "He was of middle stature and exquisitely proportioned limbs; his hair a light chestnut; his complexion betwixt pale and ruddy; his eye most penetrating though inclining to grey; his nose aquiline."

Montrose and his party passed through France and Italy, viewing the beauties of French and Italian cities and cathedrals. He was also able to attend the military academies of France, and he studied the military tactics of the Swedish King Gustavus Adolphus. Since 1618, most of Europe had been at war and people there had studied the best ways to use men and weapons in battle.

In 1636, at the age of twenty-four, Montrose returned to Scotland. He had been informed of the troubles brewing but he still stopped in London to seek an introduction to the King. This was arranged by the Marquis of Hamilton, a favourite of Charles and a man much disliked by the Scots. Hamilton had probably misinformed the King that Montrose was a conceited and ambitious young man, and Charles merely allowed the young Earl to kiss his hand before he turned away.

The Young Montrose Abroad

Montrose in 1629.

Homecoming

Signing the Covenant

Back home, James Graham quickly sided with the King's opponents. Montrose disliked bishops, disliked Charles's attitude to the Scottish nobility, and felt that although a monarch was a necessary part of government, this one had gone too far.

On 15 November 1637, Montrose was elected to the Tables, the committee set up to discuss the religious grievances. The King had no time for the Tables, and in February 1638 he tried to disband the committee. The members of the Tables knew that a Royal herald would read the King's proclamation at Edinburgh's Mercat Cross, so the King's opponents erected a scaffold nearby from where they read out their own counter-proclamation. As the Royal herald's voice was drowned out by the Tables, the young Montrose jumped on to a barrel on the scaffold. A friend commented: "James, you will not be at rest till you be lifted up there above the rest in three fathoms of rope." It was an accurate prophecy.

Montrose was one of the first to sign the National Covenant in Greyfriars kirkyard, Edinburgh, on 28 February 1638. Copies of the National Covenant were carried to every part of Scotland. Everywhere, except in the North, many signed it. The people of Scotland were making it clear that they, and not the King, were going to organise their religion.

The scene in Greyfriars kirkyard as the National Covenant was signed.

Both the Covenanters and the King expected war, and through the summer of 1638 both sides prepared for battle. One group of Highland clans, with the Campbells of Argyll taking the lead, backed the Covenant. But the King's Commissioner in Scotland, the Marquis of Hamilton, gained the support of many other clans, some for religious reasons, others simply to oppose the great clan Campbell.

The wars which followed are known as the Bishops' Wars, and they not only settled the question of religion in Scotland but led to wars in England as well — wars which decided not only matters of religion but who had the right to rule, King or Parliament.

The Covenanters quickly organised an army. A letter was signed by Montrose and others and sent round the country. It declared the need for a Covenanting army, or else the Royalist army "would force and impose a yoke of bondage upon our consciences and turn our liberty to thralldom". In each county, committees of war chose men for the army, organised weapons and raised money. Soon pikes and muskets were being distributed.

The Covenanters gave Montrose the difficult job of going to the North-East to raise support. This area had remained a staunch stronghold of support for bishops and the Episcopalian system. Try as he might, Montrose could get no backing from the city or University of Aberdeen, nor from the powerful Marquis of Huntly.

Meanwhile, the King planned to attack. He would be with the main army marching northward across the Border, while forces from Ireland would land at Dumbarton and Kintyre. In the north, the Marquis of Hamilton was to come ashore at Aberdeen and join up with the Scottish Royalists under the Marquis of Huntly. But the King's forces were ill-equipped and badly trained. Before they neared Scotland, the Covenanters had taken Dalkeith and Dumbarton. It was only Huntly and his followers in the North-East who posed any real threat. James Graham, accompanied by Field Marshal Alexander Leslie, was sent to deal with them. Leslie was an experienced soldier, having fought for years as a paid soldier in Europe.

The First Bishops' War

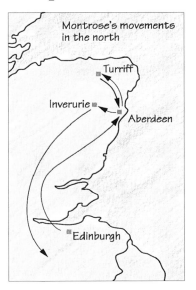

Montrose's movements in the north

Turriff

Inverurie

Aberdeen

Edinburgh

Covenanters' Action

Alexander Leslie.

The Raid of Turriff

The two men led an army towards Aberdeen. Leslie stayed there, while Montrose and a band of musketeers set out for Turriff, where he hoped to defeat Huntly and the Gordons. Finding Huntly away, Montrose and his men waited in the church, and when Huntly arrived with a stronger force, Montrose simply withdrew. The 'First Raid of Turriff' ended without bloodshed.

Aberdeen Surrenders

The Marquis of Huntly

Montrose now turned to occupy the city of Aberdeen. He rode at the head of the army, carrying a blue silk banner with the words "For God, Covenant and Country" on it, and each soldier wore a bright blue silk ribbon. The city defences collapsed and the cavalry, followed by pikemen and musketeers, entered unopposed. With trumpets sounding and drums beating, the Covenanters marched through the city and assembled on the Queen's Links — in all, 11,000 men. But they did not fight. Having made his presence felt and disbanded the city's defences, Montrose left Aberdeen for Inverurie to meet Huntly.

Montrose went to Inverurie, because he knew there would never be peace in the north until the two men had come to an agreement. Huntly, too, wanted peace. No help had yet reached him from the King, and he feared the Covenanters would plunder and pillage his lands. We have no details of their pact, but Huntly may have agreed to part of the Covenant while Montrose promised not to harass his followers.

The King's Army at the Border

But the agreement did not last. The King was now approaching the Border, and the Covenanters wanted both Leslie and Montrose in the south. Huntly was taken to Edinburgh and imprisoned. With the Covenanters' leaders away, however, the northern Royalists decided to take their chance. The first battle of the Civil Wars was a victory for the Royalists. In the 'Trot of Turriff' the Covenanters were driven out.

Aberdeen Sacked

Hearing of this, Montrose headed north again. On 25 May 1639, he entered Aberdeen with 4,000 men. This time, they showed little mercy to the townsfolk. They stole food, scoured the town for weapons and ransacked Royalist houses. They even decorated the dogs with the Covenanting blue ribbon to taunt their owners. The city was heavily fined.

In the following month the Covenanters once again prepared to go south. But Royalist troops landed at Aberdeen and the King's forces in the north were reorganised under Huntly's son, Aboyne. Montrose prepared to do battle. At the Brig o' Dee, on 18 June, the Covenanters faced the Royalists. The two armies pounded one another across the bridge for a whole day. At last the Royalist army gave up, and the Covenanters entered Aberdeen once more.

The Brig o' Dee.

The city was to suffer again. Leading Royalists were imprisoned, Aberdeen was fined £4,000 and the city had to feed and house the Covenanting army for three days. Although Montrose forbade pillage and looting, there was little he could do to stop it. It was estimated that £133,000 of damage was caused.

While in Aberdeen, Montrose received the news that the Covenanters under Leslie had defeated the King and were making peace with him at Berwick.

The Pacification of Berwick was a poor agreement. Both sides said they would disband their armies, and the King agreed to come to Edinburgh to meet both Parliament and Assembly. "God bless his Majesty and the Devil confound his Bishops," cried the Covenanters at Berwick, but still the King announced that bishops were to sit in the new Assembly. Charles invited fourteen Covenanting leaders to meet him in Berwick. Five went (including Montrose), but only to insist that the King abolish the bishops in Scotland or the Covenanters would help the King's opponents in England to get rid of the bishops there. So Charles left for London, leaving the Assembly and Parliament 'free' to demand the end of the bishops.

Peace with the King

The ruins of Berwick Castle in 1790.

The King's English Problems

The King did not see this as the end of the matter. He was determined to march against the Covenanters again, but he was desperately short of money to raise an army. To obtain money, he summoned his Parliament in England, something he had not done for eleven years. He found, however, that the English Parliament had just as many grievances against him as the Scots and would give no help until he had settled with them. Parliament was dismissed, and the King set off for the north with a very poor army.

Covenanting Victory

As Charles left York, Montrose led the Scottish army across the Border and into England. He routed the English troops at Newburn and occupied Newcastle. A truce was signed, by which the Covenanters were paid £850 a day and allowed to occupy the northern counties of England. Finally, in June 1641, the Scots (and the English Parliament) forced Charles I to agree to the laws passed by the Scottish Parliament, to remove his garrisons from Berwick and Carlisle, and to agree to discuss the reforming of the English church. The Scots were also to receive £300,000.

Parliament or King?

The Covenanters had won a bloodless victory. They had secured the right for Presbyterianism in Scotland which James Graham had fought for. But by bringing the King into conflict with the English Parliament, the Scots had gone further. The question now was who actually had the right to rule — was it Parliament or was it the King?

Chapter 5

King Stewart or King Campbell

In 1642, the King's troubles in England led to open war — Parliament versus the King. Both sides wanted Scotland as an ally. The Scottish Parliament agreed to fight on the side of the English Parliament if the English Parliament accepted the Solemn League and Covenant. The Solemn League went further than the National Covenant: it demanded that the English Church be reformed along the same lines as the Scottish Church.

Solemn League and Covenant

But Montrose did not support the Scottish Parliament and the Solemn League and Covenant. Instead, in 1644 he became the leader of a Royalist army in Scotland. Montrose was fighting against his former Covenanting allies. Had he changed sides? The answer has its roots back in the 1639 Treaty of Berwick.

Montrose — Which Side?

As we have seen, the Treaty was never really applied. The Scottish army was not disbanded, and the King still refused to recognise the Acts passed by the General Assembly and Parliament. But in July 1639 the King summoned a group of leading Covenanters to Berwick to give "an explanation of those particulars wherein they have trespassed upon his regal authority and broken their promises," and Montrose was one of only six who obeyed the King's command.

Old Inveraray Castle, seen here from the market place of Inverarary, was the seat of Archibald Campbell, Duke of Argyll.

A Meeting with the King

It was at this meeting in Berwick that Montrose really met King Charles for the first time. During the discussions, he became more and more impressed by the King. Burnet, a historian of the time, wrote that "Montrose gave His Majesty full assurances of his duty in time coming — also — he made the King fancy that he could turn the whole kingdom." Of course, this did not please Montrose's fellow Covenanters. A note was pinned to his door: *"invictus armis, verbis vincitur"* ("unconquered by arms, but conquered by words").

*Archibald Campbell,
the Earl of Argyll.*

When Montrose returned from Berwick, he soon became aware that one man above all others was trying to push for far more than the Covenanters' original demands. This was Archibald Campbell, Earl of Argyll and chief of Clan Campbell, one of the most powerful and well-organised clans in Scotland.

In the early years of the conflict between the Scots and the King, Argyll had remained aloof. He was one of the last noblemen to sign the National Covenant and he played almost no part in public life until the Glasgow Assembly of 1638. But over the following few years he became the most powerful man in Scotland.

When the Scottish Parliament met in August 1639, it was different from previous Parliaments — the bishops had been officially abolished by the Assembly. This not only meant that there were no bishops sitting as members of Parliament: there were none as members of the Lords of the Articles either. The King had always had the right to choose these Lords of the Articles, but without the bishops he would not be able to find enough supporters. Most of the nobles were Covenanters.

Argyll had a scheme, and Parliament agreed to it. He suggested that each of the two remaining Estates would elect its own Lords of the Articles — eight from the nobles and sixteen from the lairds and burgesses. This seems very reasonable today, but in 1639 it was a revolutionary change for it entirely removed the King's influence from Parliament. It also gave Argyll the chance to push forward his own interests.

Argyll's Plan

The next summer, June 1640, Parliament reassembled without the King's permission. It abolished the Lords of the Articles, and passed Acts enforcing various religious rules including the observance of the Sabbath. It also declared that Parliament must meet at least every three years, removing the King's prerogative, or right, to summon Parliament only when he wanted to.

Parliament Acts

These moves by Argyll and the Parliament worried Montrose. Charles I may not always have acted in Scotland's best interests, but was Argyll any better? And what right did he have? Already his clansmen were claiming they were "King Campbell's men, not King Stewart's". Indeed, many people wanted Argyll actually tobe crowned King. There was a poem in circulation saying:

King Campbell?

> *"I gave Argyll the praise*
> *Because all men see its treuth*
> *For he will tak geir from the Lawland men*
> *And he will tak the Crown by force;*
> *And he will cry King at Whitsunday."*

The time would come when Montrose would have to decide for himself between King Campbell and King Stewart.

It was not long before Montrose was pushed further into opposition against Argyll. Parliament granted Argyll a commission of fire and sword, giving him the right to punish his enemies by burning their lands and killing them. Parliament intended that he should destroy, once and for all, any opposition to the Covenant. In fact, Argyll took this as an opportunity to destroy his hereditary clan enemies. First to meet his wrath were the Ogilvies.

Fire and Sword

The Ogilvies were not Covenanters. They held lands in Angus and were near neighbours of Montrose. Lord Airlie, the chief, was Montrose's first cousin. To help his cousin, Montrose got to Airlie first and took the castle's surrender himself. But Argyll wanted more, and he marched through the glens at the head of an army, laying waste Ogilvy lands. When he reached Airlie Castle, he found Lord Airlie gone and only his young pregnant wife at home. The land was burned, cattle and sheep were driven off, and Lady Ogilvy was forced out of her house. The story is told in the ballad 'The Bonnie House of Airlie'.

From Airlie, Argyll continued with fire and sword into Lochaber.

By now, the rumours about Argyll's ambition to depose the King were spreading. There were also suggestions that Argyll should be made military dictator of all Scotland north of the Forth.

Airlie Castle.

From "The Bonnie House of Airlie"

"It fell on a day and a bonnie summer day
When green grew oats and barley
That there fell out a great dispute
Between Argyll and Airlie.

Lady Ogilvy looks ower her bower window
And O but she looks warely
And there she spied the great Argyll
Come to plunder the bonnie house of Airlie.

'Come down, come down, my Lady Ogilvy,
Come down and kiss me fairly.'
'O I winna kiss the false Argyll
If he shouldna leave a standing stone in Airlie.'"

This was too much for James Graham. He called together a group of moderate men, and they met at Cumbernauld House, home of the Earl of Wigtown. Montrose told them "that it was now high time to us, and all honest men who respected the Libertie of the Countrye and this caus, to joyne themselves togither to oppose those wayes of tyranny, which in effect did lead to nothing less than the ruine of Countrye, Libertie and personall fredome."

The *Cumbernauld Bond* was drawn up and signed. This was a statement that these men had signed the Covenant out of duty to their religion and country but that now this cause was suffering "by a particular and indirect practicking of a few." They were therefore prepared to join together to ensure the safety of the religion, laws and liberties of Scotland "to the hazard of our lives, fortunes and estates." In short, they were prepared to stand up to Argyll.

This does not mean that Montrose and the moderates suddenly became supporters of all King Charles's policies. They were still Covenanters and determined that the King should not impose bishops on the Church of Scotland. Before they could concentrate on the internal problems of Scotland they had to face the threat from the King.

However, once Charles was again defeated and the cause of the Covenant won, Montrose felt free to make his position clear to the King. In the summer of 1641, he wrote professing his loyalty to the crown and gave an offer of advice. The reply from the King was intercepted by Argyll's men. This was enough for Argyll, who feared Montrose and knew of the Cumbernauld Bond. James Graham was arrested and imprisoned.

'Witnesses' were arrested and tortured to produce 'evidence' (one witness was even put to death). Argyll was determined to collect enough material to charge Montrose with treason and have him executed. In fact, he could not make a case, so Montrose was just held in prison.

Montrose Against Argyll

Montrose Imprisoned

Montrose was held imprisoned in Edinburgh Castle

King Campbell

While Montrose was in prison, the King visited Scotland. Argyll appeared to give him a magnificent reception, and the King went to church and was polite to ministers. But in fact the King was doing what Argyll wanted, and Argyll was ensuring that the King's power was being replaced by his own. He saw to it that Parliament passed Acts saying that the King's ministers were to be chosen by Parliament and that nobody who had supported the King during the Bishops' Wars could hold office. It was 'King Campbell' who ruled.

Montrose could do little about this from prison. He wrote to Charles asking for an interview, but nothing happened. He wrote again, saying that he could prove that both Argyll and Charles's close friend Hamilton were traitors. The King, not knowing what else to do, showed the letter to Argyll and Hamilton.

Then a strange event, known simply as 'the Incident,' took place. A rumour ran round Edinburgh that Argyll and Hamilton were going to be murdered. The two men 'fled' from Edinburgh but absolutely nothing happened. The King, however, took all this as an indication that Argyll could be trusted, so when Argyll returned to Edinburgh Charles made him a marquis. Argyll now felt quite secure. Montrose was released from jail and the King returned to London. For the next two years, Scotland was ruled by Argyll, Covenant and Parliament.

Montrose's Dilemma

Montrose was a Covenanter who disliked bishops and was prepared to fight on that principle. He also disliked Argyll, the virtual ruler of Scotland. He apparently admired King Charles after meeting him at Berwick, but the King had done nothing to help either Montrose or himself, simply allowing himself and his power in Scotland to be overruled.

Perhaps it is not surprising that Montrose should have been such a strong opponent of Argyll. But why did he give King Charles such positive support?

Away from Strife

Montrose spent the next year at home with his family at Kincardine. It was to be the last peaceful time in his life. By now he had three sons, John, James and Robert, and a daughter, Jean. A fourth son, David, had died at the age of three. These children had been brought up by their

The Duke of Hamilton. Hamilton had been Charles I's favourite and his adviser in Scotland, and he was the person who introduced Montrose to the King. But by 1641 he was keen to keep in with the powerful Argyll.

mother, because their father was rarely at home. Another consequence of Montrose's long absences was that many of the Graham estates were badly in debt, so Montrose had to concentrate on estate management. However, he also spent a great deal of time writing poetry and thinking about his attitude to government, the Church and the rights of Parliament and the King.

Finally a Royalist

During this time, he wrote a letter which summarised and explained his position. He argued that a stable government had to have one central authority. He did not like the absolute power of a tyrant, but anarchy — or the absence of rule —was worse. Ideally, the king should be a moderate man, but a tyrannical king was better than rule by factions or groups, such as Archibald Campbell and his friends. At least a bad king eventually dies.

So when finally Civil War broke out in England and both sides looked to Scotland for help, Montrose knew on which side he stood. He was prepared to back the King against Parliamentary opponents, be they Scottish or English. And he was prepared to take positive action. Perhaps a verse from one of his own poems best describes the feelings that were to drive him over the next few years:

> *"He either fears his fate too much*
> *Or his deserts are small*
> *That dare not put it to the touch*
> *To win or lose it all."*

War in the 17th Century

Seventeenth-century armies consisted of cavalry (horsemen) and infantry (foot soldiers) armed with pikes and muskets. The Scottish government, or Covenanting, armies were trained and disciplined by such men as the Leslies, who had gained their experience fighting as mercenaries in Europe. Montrose's army was different. It had no cavalry and few guns. His Highland soldiers, dressed in their plaids, carried only dirks and swords. Montrose knew that if he was going to defeat the well-equipped Lowland troops of the Covenant, he would need to fight them on the rough ground of the Highlands, so he planned to deliver a series of attacks against Covenanting garrisons then withdraw back into the Highlands, drawing the Lowland troops after him.

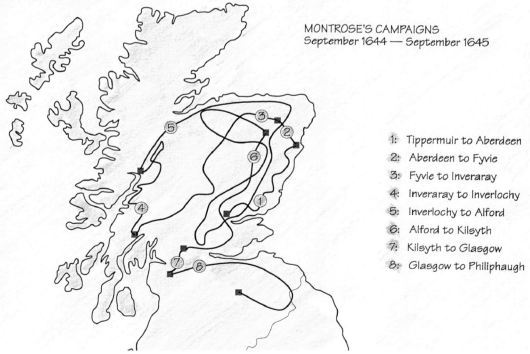

MONTROSE'S CAMPAIGNS
September 1644 — September 1645

1: Tippermuir to Aberdeen
2: Aberdeen to Fyvie
3: Fyvie to Inveraray
4: Inveraray to Inverlochy
5: Inverlochy to Alford
6: Alford to Kilsyth
7: Kilsyth to Glasgow
8: Glasgow to Philiphaugh

Chapter 6

Annus Mirabilis

In 1643, the English Parliament decided to sign the Solemn League and Covenant so that the Scottish army would fight on their side against the King. In January 1644, the Scots, under Alexander Leslie and his nephew David Leslie, marched into England to join the Parliament troops.

Throughout 1643, Montrose had been in contact with Charles. In November, he left Scotland to visit the King, now based at Oxford. Here, at last, the King rewarded him for his past loyalty, first by making him Marquis of Montrose and then, on 1 February 1644, by appointing him Lieutenant General of the King's forces in Scotland. As Lieutenant General, he was to take an English Royalist force and join up with the Royalist Gordons in the North-East. He would be joined by a force from Ireland before invading Scotland.

To England, then home

The plan failed. The King's army in England was heavily defeated at Marston Moor by the Parliamentary army and Scottish cavalry. The Gordons were also defeated. Montrose was left to enter Scotland alone and await the promised Irish force. Disguised as a groom and with only two companions, he crossed the Border and headed north to meet with friendly Royalists. He stopped at Tulliebelton, where a close kinsman, Patrick Graham (or Black Pate), lived. Here, Montrose could lie in hiding safely in the hills.

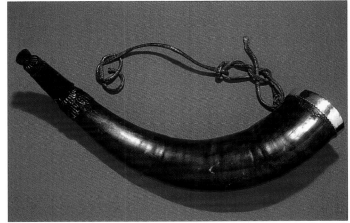

Montrose's powder horn, used for holding gunpowder for his pistol.

The Royal Standard Raised

It was to Tulliebelton that news came: the Irish, under Alasdair MacDonald, had landed in Kintyre. Montrose sent orders that they were to meet him at Blair Atholl. Here, the Irishmen, and the clans Stewart and Robertson, came together to fight for King Stewart, not for King Campbell. On 28 August 1644, Montrose raised the Royal Standard. As trumpets blared and pipes skirled, the silken banner, carried all the way from Oxford, fluttered in the breeze.

This was the opening of the campaign that made Montrose master of the Highlands — and almost made him master of Scotland. It was the campaign that was to show the brilliance of his strategy and leadership. But it was also the campaign that was to lead to the total defeat of his army and the Royalist forces in Scotland.

Supporters, Highland and Irish

Montrose at the head of his army, which he held together despite the different backgrounds of the troops. A Highland writer of the time said that Montrose's manner "quickly made a conquest of the hearts of all his followers".

Montrose's army was almost entirely made up of Highland clans and MacDonald's Irishmen. It was an assorted group, and its members were there for different reasons. Some, like the Gordons, had always been Royalist; some were Roman Catholic and therefore opposed the Presbyterian government. Others just wanted to settle old scores with the clans who supported Argyll, the Campbells and the Covenant. Alasdair MacDonald was one of these. He was a kinsman of the Earl of Antrim in northern Ireland and a son of MacDonald of Colonsay, known as Coll Ciotach. The Campbells had driven the Macdonalds from their lands

and imprisoned Coll Ciotach. The seven-foot tall Alasdair, with his 1,600 Irishmen, was really leading a band of exiled MacDonalds and Macleans, out to regain their lands and revenge Coll Ciotach's imprisonment.

What follows is a brief summary of his campaign and a look in detail at two major battles: Inverlochy, a victory; and Philiphaugh, a crushing defeat.

The map on page 30 shows the area covered by Montrose's campaign. After joining with the Irish and Royalist clans at Blair Atholl, Montrose led his army against the Covenanters. At Tippermuir on 1 September 1644, the Covenanting army fled before the charge of Highlanders and the way was open to Perth. Here Montrose was joined by his son and heir, John, Lord Graham, now aged fourteen. He was to accompany his father throughout the rest of the campaign, in case he was taken hostage. Two weeks later, Montrose entered Aberdeen, where his troops sacked and pillaged the city. Heading north, the Royalists were victorious again at Fyvie on 24 October. With the North-East settled, Montrose decided to head west to deal with the Campbells. But as he travelled round the Central Highlands, he was followed by his old enemy, Argyll.

In December, Montrose was in Inveraray, seat of the Clan Campbell, from where he drove Argyll off down Loch Fyne. From Inveraray, Montrose headed north to the Great Glen, only to find himself trapped between two armies — Campbells to the south, Mackenzie of Seaforth to the north. After a brilliant victory in February 1645 at Inverlochy, Montrose led the Royalists east again. Near Dundee he skilfully avoided a Covenanting army and headed due north. At Auldearn in May and Alford in July, the great Marquis was victorious twice more.

Montrose had won the north, but his work was not complete until he had won central Scotland, so he moved south. By the middle of August he was at Kilsyth, on the edge of the Lowlands. Here he won another victory, defeating all the Covenanting armies in Scotland. After Kilsyth, Montrose entered Glasgow and, as King Charles' Lieutenant General in Scotland, summoned a Parliament.

The Campaign

The increasingly popular basket-hilted sword which was far more manageable than the old two-handed claymore.

Defeat

But the tide was turning. Montrose's army had begun to break up as the clans grew more interested in their own affairs than the position of the King in Scotland. Alasdair MacDonald took most of his Irish forces to campaign against the Campbells in Kintyre, so Montrose set out for England with a smaller army. The King had just been decisively defeated at Naseby, and he badly needed help from the Scottish Royalists. But Montrose never reached England. At Philiphaugh, as we have seen, he was surprised by David Leslie, returning victorious from England, and decisively beaten. Montrose had won Scotland for the King and then lost it again.

Into Exile

After Philiphaugh, Montrose retreated to Blair. By March 1646, he had rebuilt an army for the King and there seemed to be some hope, but this was short-lived. David Leslie had returned with his army to England and King Charles had surrendered to him, putting himself under the control of the Covenanting army. In this position, the King ordered Montrose to disband his army. It was a hard thing for the Scottish Royalist leader to do. And it was a hard thing for his remaining troops, who would follow to the ends of the earth "a general so valiant, so skilfull and so much beloved".

James Graham, Marquis of Montrose, made his sad way to the town of Montrose on his way into exile. The Covenanters had promised him a ship, but the captain would not leave. At Stonehaven, he obtained passage on a fishing boat bound for Norway.

A view of Montrose town, from a book published in 1693.

Victory at Inverlochy

Inverlochy Castle

At Blair Castle at the beginning of December 1644 a plan was hatched to strike the Campbells in their own country. It was daring to enter the mountainous region of Argyll in midwinter, but Montrose and MacDonald both reckoned that this would surprise the Campbells. The Royalist army first attacked the Campbell stronghold at Inveraray, only to find that Argyll had fled. His clansmen followed suit and evaporated into the hills. The MacDonalds left "neither house nor hold unburned, nor corn, nor cattle that belonged to the whole name of Campbell".

The government in Edinburgh was horrified at the speed with which Montrose and Alastair MacDonald were apparently conquering Scotland. General Baillie, an experienced commander, was put in charge of the army, while Argyll recalled two Campbell regiments from Ireland. Montrose, realising that he might be trapped between the two forces, headed north for Lochaber.

But the army made slow progress. It took two days and two nights for them to cross Loch Etive with one large and three small boats, and crossing Loch Leven was almost as bad. Once into the high hills of Lochaber, they were slowed down by torrential rain and heavy snow.

Montrose's enemies believed he was trapped in the hills without food and shelter, and would be forced down into the Great Glen. They decided that Argyll would attack from the rear, Baillie from the east, and Seaforth, chief of the Mackenzies, from the north. Surrounded like this, the Royalists could not survive.

The plan would work, however, only if Montrose and MacDonald did as they expected. Instead, they took a great risk by heading back up the River Tarff and into the hills. With the weather still against them, the soldiers struggled through the hills around Ben Nevis. Then they reached the Castle of Inverlochy, near where Argyll's ship lay at anchor in Loch Linnhe, and rested for a final night before battle.

The following morning, the Royalist army could see the 3,000 of Campbell's men lined up along the high ground with the Campbell Regiment, the most highly trained of Argyll's men, in the centre. But when they advanced, Montrose's Irish troops attacked the Lowland regiments on their wings and drove them from the battlefield.

The Campbell regiment was soon surrounded. The fighting continued, and by 2 February 1645, 1,500 Campbells had fallen to the claymores and dirks of the MacDonalds. The Marquis of Argyll, who had never left his galley, fled from the area.

Montrose wrote speedily to the King "— I am in the fairest hopes of reducing this Kingdom to your Majesty's obedience — I doubt not before the end of this summer I shall be able to come to your Majesty's assistance with a brave army." But he never was able to do this.

Defeat at Philiphaugh

This picture of Montrose's defeat at Philiphaugh was painted long after the battle.

By the time Montrose had entered Glasgow after his victory at Kilsyth, the King was in desperate trouble in England. The King wanted Montrose to join him but ordered that he should wipe out the army of David Leslie before entering England. Montrose's problem was this: should he try to draw Leslie into the hills, confuse him and then pounce, a course that would take weeks; or should he risk taking his small force south to join up with Lowland Royalists and then attack. He decided on the latter course, as two of the greatest Border lords, Roxburgh and Hume, promised him 2,000 men if he came south in person. But when Montrose arrived at Kelso with his army, which was now much smaller, he discovered no troops. Instead, Roxburgh and Hume, fearing defeat, had turned and joined Leslie's army. It would be impossible now for James Graham to face this force and continue south. He would have to retreat to Glasgow.

The army camped for the night, with the cavalry at Selkirk and the infantry nearby at Philiphaugh on the River Yarrow. But in the dark, Leslie's army surrounded the Royalists at Philiphaugh. By early morning, the infantry were fighting for their lives. The cavalry were coming up from Selkirk and could do little to help. It was hardly surprising that 600 men of the Royalist army could not hold against 6,000 trained men of the Covenanting army. Soon, 400 infantry and 50 cavalry were dead. The remainder surrendered when they were promised mercy. Montrose himself managed to escape, hoping that once again the chance would come to raise an army for the King.

The victors of Philiphaugh had not finished. The camp-followers, wives and children, were massacred. The few soldiers who escaped were rounded up and butchered in the hills. Those who surrendered were marched to Glasgow, put on trial before Parliament, then executed. In the name of religion and the Covenant, there was no mercy.

Chapter 7

Exile

Montrose was to spend four years in exile working for a single cause: restoring the monarchy to both Scotland and England. They were years of hoping, waiting, travelling, planning and disappointment.

To Paris and the English Court

After arriving in Bergen in September 1646, James Graham set out "by a wild and difficult route across the rugged mountain ranges buried in perpetual ice and snow" for Christiana (modern Oslo) and Copenhagen. At Copenhagen he hoped to talk to — and obtain help from — Christian IV, King of Denmark and uncle of Charles I. But Christian was in Germany, so Montrose travelled on to Hamburg, where he waited in vain before finally deciding that he must go to Paris to make contact with the exiled English Court there. He felt sure they must want to restore Charles I to all his power.

The Court, led by Charles's wife, Henrietta Maria, was bright and frivolous. Montrose arrived there in March 1647, only to find that his offer to lead an army was shunned. Maybe the English in Paris were simply realistic and felt that an invasion of Britain on behalf of Charles would simply be futile. At all events, it seemed that the trivial affairs of the Court were more important to the English exiles than the position of their King.

Henrietta Maria, wife of King Charles.

Charles I Imprisoned

Oliver Cromwell.

The Engagement

While Montrose was ignored by the English in Paris, the French sought him out. They had heard of his military victories and would have liked to recruit him as a leader in their army. He was offered command of the Scots in France, a lieutenant-governorship of the French army, the captaincy of the gendarmerie, and the rank of Marshal of France. If Montrose had accepted these high honours, he could have had a great career at the head of the French army, but he turned all this down; as his only aim and object was to win back Scotland and England for the King.

Montrose's difficulty in trying to gain support from Henrietta Maria and her court was complicated by events in Britain. During 1646 the King had become a prisoner of the Scots army. In January 1647 the Scots handed him over to the English Parliament. Parliament, in turn, was forced to hand him over to the army of Oliver Cromwell, who was now, in effect, the ruler of England. Charles was imprisoned at Carisbrooke Castle on the Isle of Wight.

Many Scots were now beginning to agree with Montrose that, while the King had undoubtedly gone too far, replacing his rule with the fanaticism of Oliver Cromwell was probably worse. On 29 December 1647, three leading Scots (Loudoun, Lanark and Lauderdale) signed an *Engagement* with the King at Carisbrooke. They agreed to send a Scottish army to release the King and restore him to London in return for the establishment of Presbyterianism in England for a trial period of three years.

The 'Engagers' communicated with Henrietta Maria but made it clear that they wanted nothing to do with Montrose. He was still considered an enemy of Scotland. If Montrose had ever had a chance of obtaining support in Paris it had now gone.

Disappointed, Montrose left France and set out across Europe to raise a private army. Ahead of him went his fame, for recently a book recounting his campaigns, written by his chaplain George Wishart, had been published in Holland. At Prague, Montrose met the Holy Roman Emperor Ferdinand, who gave him the right to raise troops through the Empire. Ferdinand also suggested that his brother, Archduke Leopold, Governor of the Spanish Netherlands, could help him. Much of Germany was being fought over, so Montrose took a long and difficult route from Prague to the Netherlands, finally reaching Brussels by way of Cracow, Danzig, Denmark and Holland. Again his hopes were dashed. Archduke Leopold had just been defeated by the French at Lens. He had no army left to give to the Scottish Royalist.

At the same time, Montrose heard that the Engagement had failed. The Scottish army, marching through England to release the King, had been heavily defeated at Preston by the army of Oliver Cromwell.

This last piece of news was probably welcome to the Marquis. Surely now Henrietta Maria and the Prince of Wales would have to recognise that he was the only hope left to the Royalists. In fact, Charles, Prince of Wales, did agree to meet him. Montrose was delighted: on 28 January 1649 he wrote to the Prince, "If your Highness shall vouchsafe a little faith unto your loyal servants, and stand at guard with others, your affairs can soon be whole."

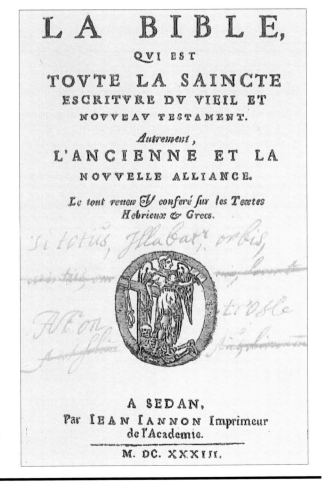

The title page of
Montrose's French bible.

A King Executed

Two days later, King Charles I was beheaded by the English Parliament. When Montrose heard the news, he fainted. For two whole days he shut himself in his room. Later his chaplain found the following scribbled lines. They were to become the resistance poem of the Royalists for the next ten years:

> *"Great, good, and just, could I but rate*
> *My grief, and thy too rigid fate,*
> *I'd weep the world in such a strain*
> *As it should deluge once again.*
> *But since thy loud-tongued blood demands supplies*
> *More from Briareus' hands than Argus' eyes,*
> *I'll sing dirge with trumpet sounds*
> *And write thine epitaph with blood and wounds."*

> *(Montrose is saying that if he could allow his grief at the King's fate to flow naturally, his weeping would flood the world. But the King's death demands military action rather than tears, so the song of mourning will be sung by war trumpets, and the epitaph written in blood.)*

A new King?

But Montrose did not mourn long. Three weeks later he kissed the hand of his new king, Charles II, at The Hague and offered to launch an invasion of Scotland, to raise the clans and reconquer the country as he had done five years earlier for Charles's father. The 18-year-old King willingly accepted the offer and made Montrose Lieutenant General of Scotland.

The Execution of Charles I.

Both the King and Montrose had acted without knowing what was going on in Scotland. In fact, the Scottish government, under Argyll, had been infuriated by the execution of Charles I, which had been done by the English without any consent of the Scottish Parliament. Argyll and Parliament proclaimed Charles II King and sent a party of ministers over to The Hague to ask Charles to return to Edinburgh. But he was asked to return on their terms.

What was the young King to do? If he accepted the terms of the Scots, which included agreeing to the Covenant and denouncing his father and mother, he would be King in little more than name. Argyll would be the real ruler of Scotland. If he accepted Montrose's offer, he might be able to rule as he wished, but he might lose everything. Could Montrose really win Scotland for the King when he had failed to do so before?

For the next few months, while Charles II tried to make up his mind, James Graham enjoyed being at the court in The Hague as a guest of Elizabeth, the exiled Queen of Bohemia and sister of Charles I. The 'Winter Queen' had been driven with her husband from Bohemia thirty years earlier. She was famed for her wit and charm. Her two daughters, Louise and Sophie, were with their mother at the Hague, and years later, Sophie wrote of the months Montrose spent with them:

> "Since he was a brave soldier and a man of high merit, he thought nothing impossible to his management and courage. He was sure he could restore the young King and his Majesty would make him Viceroy of Scotland and if he did him so great a service, the King could not refuse him the hand of my sister Princess Louise."

Montrose was obviously confident that he could win Scotland. Did he also have time, as this passage suggests, to fall in love? It is possible. His wife Magdalen was dead. Princess Louise was twenty-seven, apparently beautiful and clever, and fond of painting. Perhaps it was because of her that Montrose had his portrait painted by her master, Gerrard Honthorst, the court painter. We shall never know, but the portrait of 'the Cavalier in Mourning' remains.

Argyll or Montrose?

Montrose and the Princess

The Cavalier in mourning.

The King's Support at last

In May 1649, despite the long lectures of Argyll's ministers, Charles II apparently decided to support Montrose's plan. He gave the Marquis the right to negotiate on his behalf with foreign rulers, to raise troops, and to command all the forces of Scotland by land and sea.

Bidding farewell to Elizabeth of Bohemia and her daughters, Montrose set out for Germany, Denmark and Sweden to raise troops. In July, he sent an appeal to Scotland to beg loyal people to rise against those who had "sold their sovereign into death and yet dig in his grave".

Charles's Indecision

Infuriated, Argyll and his party promised a terrible vengeance should Montrose land in Scotland. They also renewed their pressure on Charles to come to terms with them. Charles began to give in to them. He continued to write and encourage Montrose, instructing him to invade Scotland, but at the same time he was discussing agreements with Argyll's men. This made life very difficult for Montrose. How could the Kings of Denmark and Sweden really believe that Charles II wanted Montrose to raise an army to invade Scotland when the King was obviously coming to terms with Argyll?

After months of delays and waiting for news, Montrose set sail from Gothenburg in March 1650. Still convinced he was doing the only right thing, he must have known the odds were against him. Argyll had Scotland in his control. By now he probably had the King in his control too.

Chapter 8

The Last Campaign

Montrose had chosen the Orkney Isles as a base for his attack. They were far away from the Covenanters' control, yet near enough for him to join up with the Royalist Highland chiefs.

But fate seemed to be against Montrose. He had managed to raise only a small force in Sweden; a storm scattered his ships, and the ammunition vessels sank before arriving in Orkney. In Orkney, he heard the official news that the King was coming to terms with Argyll and the Covenanters. Yet the King still wrote to Montrose commanding him to carry on with his campaign. The king added that:

> *"...we doubt not but all our loyal subjects of Scotland will cordially join with you."*

He also sent Montrose the Order of the Garter.

Did Charles really think that his "loyal subjects" would join Montrose, who was trying to raise the clans, while Argyll had put a price of £30,000 on his head in the King's name? Montrose probably knew that failure was likely, but he still wrote back telling the King that he was prepared to abandon his life for the King's interests.

In early April, 1650, James Graham, with his small army of Danes and Orcadians, crossed the Pentland Firth. From Thurso they planned to make for Inverness to join up with the Mackenzies. They never reached Inverness. By 25 April, the force had reached the valley of Carbisdale in Strath Oykel. Here they stopped and built defences while waiting for the Monroes and Rosses to join them from the west.

Orkney

Rout at Carbisdale

On 27 April, disaster struck when they faced a cavalry charge from a Covenanting force under Colonel Strachan. The Orcadians, who had never seen cavalry, simply flung down their arms and fled. Montrose and a small band of men retreated into a wood, from where he sent a messenger to tell the Monroes and Rosses to hurry. When they arrived and saw the Orcadians fleeing from Strachan's cavalry, they decided to join the winning side, and they turned on the remaining Royalist forces.

This seemed to be a repetition of all that had happened at Philiphaugh. Montrose's army had been routed, and while Montrose himself managed to escape, the Covenanters were determined to round up every single remaining Royalist and to show no mercy.

Escape to the West and Betrayal

Montrose and two companions quickly fled from the scene of battle. Perhaps if they could reach Thurso they could re-form and start again. The weather was appalling. The thick mist and rain made it impossible for the men to know in which direction they were going. Occasionally they would hear thudding hooves as Strachan's men rode out to kill any survivors. They separated, and Montrose was left to find his own way. On the fourth day he was near Loch Assynt, MacLeod country. At Ardvreck Castle on Loch Assynt, Montrose was captured and handed over to the Covenanters.

Ardvreck Castle in the late 19th century.

There are two stories about the capture of Montrose. One is that Neil MacLeod of Ardvreck Castle found Montrose wandering on the moors, arrested him and held him while he sent word to Strachan — the straightforward thing to do for a man who was loyal to the government in power.

The other story is more devious. It was said that Montrose arrived at MacLeod's castle, hungry and weary. MacLeod took him in and treated him with great kindness, even promising to help him back to Thurso. But the story goes on that MacLeod and his wife wanted the Government's ransom of £30,000, so while they feasted and rested James Graham, they sent word to Strachan.

When Montrose realised what was happening, he offered MacLeod a great sum of money to release him. When this failed, he begged MacLeod to kill him then and there so that he might not die in Edinburgh at the hands of his enemies. MacLeod, however, made sure that Montrose was handed over alive to Strachan

Whichever story is true, the latter is the one that has gone down in Highland tradition, and the name of Neil MacLeod of Assynt is that of a traitor. These are the words of the Gaelic poet Iain Lom:

> *"You and your father-in-law, that goodman of Lemlair, although you should both be hanged it would not be sufficient blood-price for my loss.*

> *You are a stripped branch of the perfumed apple tree without fruit or honour or comeliness, ever engaged in murdering one another you are the leavings of sword thrusts and dirks. The death should be about you, despicable one, for you have sinfully sold the truth for Leith meal, most of which had gone sour."*

It was a long road to the Edinburgh Tolbooth and the gallows. On 5 May, Montrose was taken from Ardvreck to Tain and into the hands of General Leslie. Montrose "sat upon a little shelty horse, without a saddle, but a quilt of rags and straw and pieces of rope for stirrups; his feet fastened under the horses belly with a tether; a bit halter for a bridle". It must have been a painful journey for a man suffering from neglected wounds and a raging fever.

The party journeyed by way of Elgin, Keith and Fordoun to his father-in-law's castle at Kinnaird. Ahead travelled a herald proclaiming, "Here comes James Graham, a traitor to his country." At Kinnaird he was allowed to see his younger sons, James and Robert, aged fourteen and twelve. His eldest son and wife were both dead.

From Kinnaird it was on to Dundee, where "the whole town expressed a good deal of sorrow for his condition; and furnished him with clothes and all other things suitable to his place, birth and person". Then the company travelled through Fife and took a ship for Leith. It was Saturday, 18 May 1650.

The Last Journey

Montrose's long road to Edinburgh took him from the far north through Dingwall, Beauly and Inverness to Kinnaird Castle, then on to Fife and the ship for Leith.

Arrival in Edinburgh

Parliament had already decided what was to be done with James Graham. He was met at Leith by the magistrates and led to the entrance of Edinburgh at the Canongate. Here the officers of justice, the hangman, and the hangman's cart, awaited him. After he had read Parliament's sentence, he climbed on to the cart, where he was tied to a high seat with his arms pinioned behind him. Slowly the procession moved up the Canongate, past the houses of the nobility, and into the High Street towards the Tolbooth. The streets were crowded with the poor of Edinburgh, the black-coated ministers, and the ordinary citizens. Parliament bribed people to throw stones at the helpless Marquis, but according to one witness, "there appeared in him such majesty, courage, modesty, that those common women who had lost their husbands and children in his wars, who were hired to stone him were so astonished and moved that their intended curse turned into tears and prayers".

Moray House in the Canongate, from where Argyll watched Montrose on his way to the tolbooth

The Covenanting nobles had gathered in the houses along the Canongate to watch the procession of their defeated enemy. Argyll was in the house of Lord Moray, celebrating the marriage of his son Lord Lorne to Moray's daughter. Montrose looked Argyll straight in the eye before the shutters were quickly closed. Then on up to the Mercat Cross, where the gallows were waiting, and into the Tolbooth, Montrose's final prison and resting place.

Prisoner of Conscience

The prisoner was given little peace. Church ministers and Parliament men questioned him and taunted him. They accused him of pride and of causing war and bloodshed. He was accused of having disowned the Covenant. He replied that he still owned and adhered to the Covenant, and that he had never intended to advance the cause of the bishops or their church.

On Monday, Montrose was taken to Parliament House to hear formally the charges against him. Even though he knew he had no chance to save his life, he defended himself, saying, "My care has always been to walk as became a good Christian and a loyal subject." The sentence was read.

James Graham, Marquis of Montrose, was to be hanged at the Cross, beheaded and quartered. His head was to be displayed upon the Tolbooth and his legs and arms at the gates of Stirling, Perth and Aberdeen. If he repented, his body would be buried in Greyfriars kirkyard; if not, in the criminal's pit on the Burgh Muir. The date for the execution was the next day, Tuesday, 21 May 1650. He did not repent.

Montrose dressed carefully that morning. He wore "fine scarlet laid over with silver and lace, his hat in his hand, his hands and cuffs exceeding rich, his delicate white gloves on his hands, his stockings of silk, his shoes with ribbons on his feet. To be short, nothing was here deficient to honour his poor carcass, more becoming a bridegroom than a criminal going to the gallows."

Once dressed, he had a short walk to the gallows. By now Montrose was completely at ease, as the lines written in his cell show. In this poem, he talks of how little he cares what happens to his body, since he knows God will judge him to have done right.

> *"Let them bestow on every airt a limb*
> *Open all my veins, that I may swim*
> *To Thee my Saviour, in that Crimson Lake,*
> *Then place my pur-boiled head upon a stake*
> *Scatter my ashes, throw them in the air;*
> *Lord (since Thou know'st where all these atoms are)*
> *I'm hopeful, once Thou'll recollect my dust*
> *And confident Thou'll raise me with the just."*

To the crowd he bid farewell with the words: "I shall pray for you all. I leave my soul to God, my service to my Prince, my goodwill to my friends, and my name and charity to you all." He gave the hangman four pieces of gold and climbed the ladder "in a very stately manner". His last words were "May almighty God have mercy on this afflicted country." The executioner put the noose around Montrose's neck. Montrose then gave a hand signal and was pushed off.

An English witness described how Montrose's face never changed, and added: "He has overcome more men by his death than he would have done if he had lived. For I never saw a sweeter carriage in a man in all my life."

Sentence Passed

Execution

Montrose's sword.

Postscript

On Saturday, 11 May 1661, a great state funeral was held in Edinburgh. People crowded on the stairs and balconies of the houses to watch the procession taking the great Marquis of Montrose to his grave in the High Kirk of St Giles. Archibald Campbell, Marquis of Argyll, did not watch. He lay imprisoned in Edinburgh Castle under sentence of death.

What had happened in the eleven years since Montrose's death? Why were the severed remains of his body now gathered together and buried while his enemy awaited execution?

Charles II.

Charles II had not remained King of Scots for long. He soon recognised Argyll's ambitions and left the country. By 1654, Oliver Cromwell and the English had defeated Scotland and forced a union of the two countries. Cromwell ruled as Lord Protector. Argyll, quickly realising he would never rule Cromwell, did everything he could to cooperate with the invader. Soon "the hate of the country was heavy upon him".

Finally, in 1660, Charles II was restored to the thrones of England and Scotland. What Montrose had fought for at last was won. Charles II knew now who was his enemy in Scotland and who had been his friend.